Reptiles

KINGFISHER

LONDON & NEW YORK

Distributed in the U.S. by Macmillan, 175 Fifth Ave., New York, NY 10010

First published as *Kingfisher Young Knowledge: Reptiles* in 2006
Additional material produced for Kingfisher by Discovery Books Ltd.

Library of Congress Cataloging-in-Publication data has been applied for.

ISBN: 978-0-7534-6605-6

Kingfisher books are available for special promotions and premiums.
For details contact: Special Markets Department, Macmillan, 175 Fifth Ave., New York, NY 10010.

For more information, please visit www.kingfisherbooks.com

Printed in China
1 3 5 7 9 8 6 4 2
1TR/0511/WKT/UG/140MA

Note to readers: the website addresses listed in this book are correct at the time of going to print. However, due to the ever-changing nature of the Internet, website addresses and content can change. Websites can contain links that are unsuitable for children. The publisher cannot be held responsible for changes in website addresses or content or for information obtained through a third party. We strongly advise that Internet searches be supervised by an adult.

Acknowledgments
The publisher would like to thank the following for permission to reproduce their material. Every care has been taken to trace copyright holders. However, if there have been unintentional omissions or failure to trace copyright holders, we apologize and will, if informed, endeavor to make corrections in any future edition.
b = bottom, *c* = center, *l* = left, *t* = top, *r* = right

Photographs: *cover* Shutterstock Images; 1*bc* Alamy/FLPA/Chris Mattison; 3*bc* Jurgen & Christine Sohns/FLPA; 4–5*c* Corbis/Rod Patterson; 6–7*bl* Getty Images/Marvin E. Newman; 7*t* Getty Images/Jeffrey L. Rotman; 7*crb* Kingfisher/Art Bank; 8*b* Photolibrary.com/OSF/Tui De Roy; 9*tr* Photolibrary.com/OSF/Mark Hamblin; 9*cl* Corbis/Frank Lukasseck; 9*br* Photolibrary.com/OSF/Robin Bush; 10*cl* NHPA/Daniel Heuclin; 10–11*cl* Corbis/Michael & Patricia Fogden; 11*br* Cyril Ruoso/JH Editorial/Minden Pictures/FLPA; 12*bl* Getty Images/Richard Coomber; 12–13*t* Yossi Eshbol/FLPA; 13*b* Heidi & Hans-Juergen Koch/Minden Pictures/FLPA; 14*bl* John Cancalosi/Naturepl.com; 15*t* Corbis/George McCarthy; 15*bl* David Kjaer/Naturepl.com; 16*b* Corbis/John Conrad; 17*t* Getty Images/Peter Weber; 17*cr* Getty Images/Dr. Dennis Kunkel; 17*b* Corbis/Joe McDonald; 18*bl* Photolibrary.com/OSF; 19*tr* Barry Mansell/Naturepl.com; 19*br* Anup Shah/Naturepl.com; 20*b* Corbis/Nigel J. Dennis; 21*t* Getty Images/Paul Chesley; 21*cl* Corbis/ Michael & Patricia Fogden; 21*c* Alamy/IT Stock Free/Dynamics Graphics Group; 22*bl* Tui De Roy/Minden Pictures/FLPA; 23*cl* Flip Nicklin/Minden Pictures/FLPA; 23*b* Photolibrary.com/OSF/Tobias Bernhard; 24*c* Pete Oxford/Minden Pictures/FLPA; 25*tr* Photolibrary.com/OSF/Stan Osolinski; 25*cl* NHPA/Stephen Dalton; 25*br* NHPA/Stephen Dalton; Photolibrary.com/OSF/Ingo Arndt; 27*tl* Patricia & Michael Fogden/Minden Pictures/ FLPA; 27*cr* NHPA/Daniel Heuclin; 27*br* Photolibrary.com/OSF/Michael Fogden; 28*b* Photolibrary.com/OSF/Michael Fogden; 29*cl* D. Zingel Eichhorn/FLPA; 29*cr* Rupert Barrington/Naturepl.com; 30*b* Michael & Patricia Fogden/Minden Pictures/FLPA; 31*tr* Getty Images/Steve Winter; 31*br* NHPA/Laurie Campbell; 32*b* Getty Images/Bill Curtsinger; 33*tl* Chris Mattison/FLPA; 33*cr* NHPA/Martin Harvey; 34–35*bc* Corbis/Rod Patterson; 35*tr* Getty Images/Altrendo Nature; 35*br* Getty Images/Theo Allofs; 36*bl* John Cancalosi/Naturepl.com; 37*tr* Photolibrary.com/OSF/Dani Jeske; 37*b* Getty Images/Theo Allofs; 38*bl* NHPA/Anthony Bannister; 38–39*c* Photolibrary.com/OSF/Tobias Bernhard; 39*tr* ZSSD/Minden Pictures/FLPA; 39*br* Getty Images/Joel Sartore; 40*cl* NHPA/Daniel Heuclin; 40*br* Still Pictures/ Lynda Richardson; 40–41*c* Corbis/Philip Gould; 48*t* Shutterstock Images/AZPworldwide; 48*b* Shutterstock Images/Heiko Kiera; 49*t* Shutterstock Images/Joern; 49*b* Shutterstock Images/Matthew Cole; 52*t* Shutterstock Images/ MISHELLA; 52*b* Shutterstock Images/Fedor Selivanov; 53*t* Shutterstock Images/Rich Carey; 53*b* Shutterstock Images/Karen Givens; 56*t* Wikimedia/Hans Hilleware

Commissioned photography on pages 42–47 by Andy Crawford
Thank you to models Dilvinder Dilan Bhamra, Cherelle Clarke,
Madeleine Roffey, and William Sartin

Reptiles

Belinda Weber

KINGFISHER
NEW YORK

Contents

What is a reptile?

Reptiles are a group of animals with tough, scaly skin. They have a skeleton and a backbone. There are more than 8,000 different kinds of reptiles.

Tough and scaly

Reptile skin is covered in thin, protective plates called scales, which are stronger than normal skin. Alligators have skin covered in thick, horny plates.

Water features
Crocodiles live near water. Like water birds, they have webbed feet to help them swim.

Different homes
All reptiles are suited to where they live. Alligators' bodies are designed for moving both in and out of water.

Prehistoric reptiles
Reptiles have prehistoric ancestors. Archelon was a giant sea reptile related to modern-day turtles.

Different types

Reptiles come in many shapes and sizes. Largest of all are the saltwater crocodiles, which grow to about 23 feet (7 meters) long. Reptiles can be put into four different groups.

Reptiles with shells

Turtles, terrapins, and tortoises belong to this group. They all have hard, bony shells to protect their soft bodies inside.

Lizards and snakes

This is the largest reptile group. There are more than 3,000 different species of lizards and snakes found all over the world.

The crocodilians

Alligators, crocodiles, caimans, and gavials belong to this group. They all can move quickly over land, but most are found wallowing in water.

A group of their own

Tuataras are the only members of the smallest reptile group. They are found only on a few tiny islands off the coast of New Zealand.

Temperature control

Reptiles are cold-blooded, which means their bodies stay at the same temperature as their surroundings. They lie in the sun to warm up and hide in the shade to cool down. Once warm, they hunt for food.

Too cool to move

When some reptiles, such as rattlesnakes, find it too cold, they hibernate (go into a deep sleep) until warmer weather returns.

Staying warm

Chameleons bask in the sun to heat up their blood. Reptiles need to be warm in order to hunt and digest their food.

Cooling off

A crocodile cools down by "gaping" its mouth very wide. Or it can take a dip in the river or lie in the shade.

Reptile skin

All animals need skin to stop them from drying out in the sun. Skin also helps protect an animal's insides from injury.

Spiky skin

Some reptiles, such as iguanas, have spikes down their backs to protect them from predators. These tough scales are made of keratin—the same material as our fingernails.

Smooth skin

Burrowing reptiles such as sandfish have smooth, flexible scales. These lie flat against the skin to help the animal slide into its burrow.

Growing bigger

A snake sheds its skin as it grows. It wiggles until it is free of the old skin. This is called sloughing.

Reptile senses

Senses help animals understand their world. All animals use their senses to find food, stay safe, and find a mate. Most reptiles can see, hear, and smell, and some can "taste" things in the air.

eardrum

Listening lizards

Lizards do not have soft ears on the outside of their head like we do. Instead, they have an eardrum on each side of their head to pick up sounds.

Tasting smells

Many snakes and lizards flick
out their tongues to "taste" the
air. A sense organ in the mouth
works out what the tastes are.

Looking all around

A chameleon can
move each eye on its
own. This means the
animal can look in two
different directions at
the same time.

Foot functions

Reptiles exist all over the world, so they live in many different habitats. Their feet have evolved and adapted to suit their way of living. Some climb and some dig, while others can grip onto branches.

Spreading the weight
Giant tortoises have huge feet. As they clamber over sandy ground, their big feet help spread out their weight so that they do not sink.

Gripping pads

This gecko is an excellent climber. Tiny, hooklike hairs on its feet (shown on the right) allow it to cling onto almost anything.

Walking on water

Basilisks have wide feet and broad, scaly toes. They move quickly on these special feet to prevent them from sinking as they run across water.

Fangs and teeth

Some reptiles are small and hunt insects. Larger ones eat meatier creatures, such as mammals. All reptiles have a mouth and teeth suited to catching and eating their prey.

Snapping jaws
Alligator snapping turtles have sharp edges to their strong jaws. They snap them shut to slice prey into bite-size pieces

Fold-away fangs

This rattlesnake has two sharp, hollow teeth called fangs, which unfold for biting. Poison is pumped through the fangs to kill their prey.

Catching fish

The mouth of the Ganges gavial is lined with small, sharp teeth. The teeth fit together tightly to stop fish from getting away.

Moving on land

All reptiles have a bony skeleton that helps give their body its shape. Many have four legs, but snakes and some lizards do not have any legs. Most reptiles can move quickly to hunt or escape from danger.

Handling the heat

The Namib sand gecko has long legs. When it gets too hot, the gecko pushes up on these legs to lift its belly clear of the scorching desert sands.

Sidewinding

Sidewinder rattlesnakes wiggle and loop their body along the hot ground. This way, only a small part of their body touches the baking-hot sand at any one time.

Inside a snake

A snake's skeleton has a flexible backbone with ribs attached. It is very bendable, so a snake can coil up or wrap around things.

Moving **in water**

Some reptiles live in water, while others swim to find food or to cool themselves down. All reptiles breathe air, so even those living in water have to surface from time to time to take in air.

Finding food

Marine iguanas are the world's only ocean lizards. They feed on seaweed and can stay underwater for about 20 minutes.

Graceful swimmers

Green sea turtles beat their front flippers like wings and use their back ones to steer. Their smooth shells help them move in water.

Powerful swimmers

Saltwater crocodiles swish their long tails from side to side to push them through water. Their legs help them steer.

Moving in trees

Many reptiles are good at climbing. Tree-living geckos have special foot pads for gripping slippery leaves, while some snakes have ridged scales for clinging onto branches.

Clinging on

Tree snakes have long, strong bodies. They wrap themselves around branches and reach out into the open to look for predators or prey.

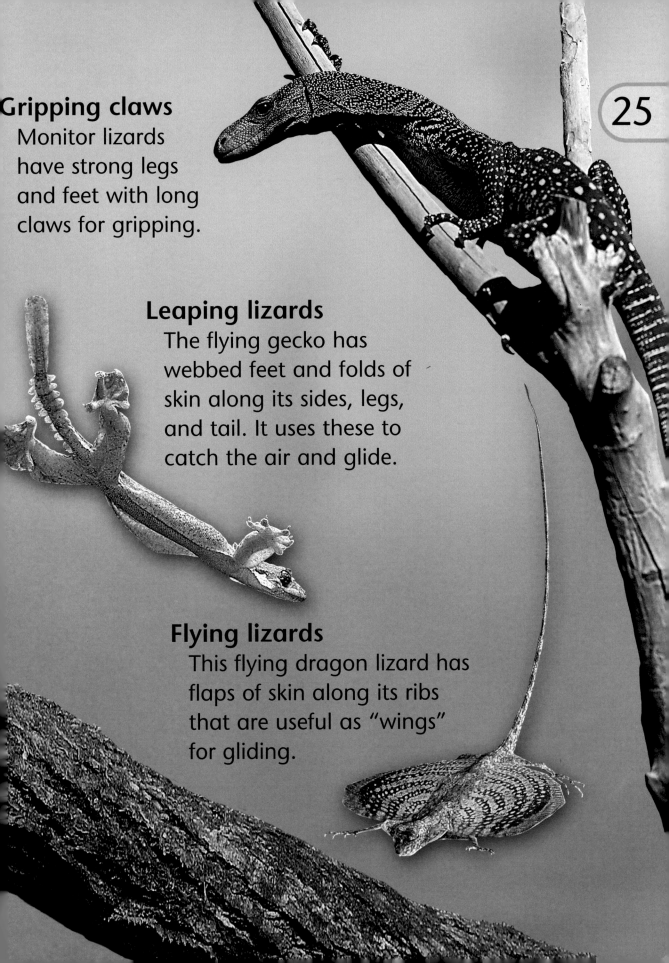

Gripping claws

Monitor lizards have strong legs and feet with long claws for gripping.

Leaping lizards

The flying gecko has webbed feet and folds of skin along its sides, legs, and tail. It uses these to catch the air and glide.

Flying lizards

This flying dragon lizard has flaps of skin along its ribs that are useful as "wings" for gliding.

Finding food

Although some lizards eat only plants, most reptiles are carnivores, which means that they hunt other animals. Some reptiles, such as crocodiles, have a varied diet, while others eat just one type of food.

Elastic tongue
Chameleons grip onto branches. They have a long, sticky tongue, which they shoot out at high speed to catch any insects that they see.

Eating frogs' eggs

When the cat-eyed snake finds a cluster of frogs' eggs, it slurps up the whole sticky mass.

Leafy dinner

The Solomon Island skink is strictly a plant eater. It climbs trees to feast on the fresh green leaves.

Fresh eggs

The African egg-eating snake swallows eggs whole. It pierces the shells in its throat so that it does not spill what is inside.

Finding a mate

When animals are ready to breed, they find a mate. Some reptiles use smell to attract a partner, while others use colors, sounds, and even dancing. Many males fight to win a female.

Bright throat

This male anole lizard puffs up its colorful throat and nods its head up and down. This shows females that he is ready to mate and warns away rival males.

Breeding dance

Speckled rattlesnake males prove their strength by wrestling. They are venomous (poisonous), but they do not bite each other.

Wrestling match

Using their tails for support, male monitor lizards rear up on their back legs and fight rival males. The weaker male gives up.

Reptile eggs

Most reptiles lay eggs with soft yet tough shells. The egg's yolk provides the developing young with food. The shell protects it from outside conditions.

A turtle nest

This olive ridley sea turtle is laying about 100 eggs into a hole that she has dug in the sand. She will return to the ocean after burying them.

Breaking out

Developing snakes grow an "egg tooth" on the tip of their upper jaw. They use it to pierce the egg's shell when they are ready to hatch.

Live babies

Some snakes and lizards give birth to live young. This lizard's Arctic home is too cold for eggs.

Growing up

Baby reptiles usually look like small versions of the adults. They are able to catch their own food as soon as they hatch. Some begin by eating smaller prey than the adults eat.

Digging for freedom
Newly hatched olive ridley sea turtles dig their way out of their sandy nests. They crawl as quickly as they can toward the ocean.

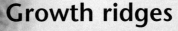

Growth ridges

As a tortoise's shell grows, another ridge is added to the patterns. People can figure out the animal's age by counting the ridges.

ridges

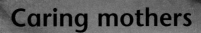

Caring mothers

Although a fierce predator, this female Nile crocodile is a caring mother. She gently scoops her babies into her mouth to keep them safe.

Staying safe

Reptiles use many different tricks to stay hidden while out hunting or while resting. If startled, some pretend to be dead. Others show that they are poisonous by being brightly colored.

Armor plating

An armadillo lizard has sharp, spiny growths on its skin. When threatened, the lizard grabs its tail and curls up into a spiky ball.

Hiding in leaves

Gaboon vipers have mottled patterns on their skin. This helps them stay hidden among leaf litter.

gaboon viper _____

Too big to eat?

Frilled lizards have a flap of skin around their heads that they can raise up. This makes them look bigger and scarier if a predator attacks.

Dragons and devils

Lizards are the most successful group of reptiles, and they live in many different places. Some have developed into big and fierce predators. Others are much smaller and live in trees or even underground.

Dragons with beards

When threatened, the bearded dragon puffs up a spiky flap of skin under its chin. This makes it look too big to eat.

Big dragons

Komodo dragons are the largest of all lizards. They can catch goats and pigs, but they usually eat carrion (dead animals).

Thorny devils

A thorny devil's spines and
prickles protect the animal
from attack. They also
catch dew for the
lizard to drink.

Using poisons

Many reptiles use venom (poison) to kill prey. Venom can affect the nervous system, the tissues of the body, or even the blood. Venomous reptiles may also use these poisons for self-defense.

Spitting cobras
A spitting cobra sprays venom out of its mouth. It aims for its enemy's eyes. The poison is very painful and can cause blindness.

A poisonous bite

Gila monsters are one of two venomous lizard species. Their venomous saliva (spit) poisons prey as they bite and chew.

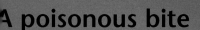

Swimming snakes

Sea snakes are the most venomous snakes in the world. They can swim underwater for up to five hours.

Noisy rattles

Rattlesnakes twitch the loose scales at the end of their tail to make a rattling sound. This warns potential predators that their bite is poisonous.

A future for reptiles

Many reptiles are in danger or face becoming extinct. We must learn how our actions may harm reptiles and do more to take care of them.

Harmful trade

Many reptiles are killed for their skins. The skins are then used to make wallets, boots, and belts, or souvenirs for tourists.

Tracking reptiles

This loggerhead turtle is being fitted with a radio transmitter. Scientists will monitor its movements so that they can learn more about this creature.

Returning to the wild

This alligator was once caught and sold as a pet. Luckily, it was rescued and returned to its real home.

Lizard cape

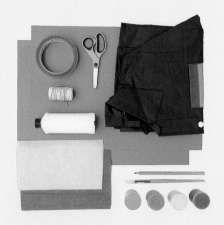

Make your own frilled cape

The Australian frilled lizard defends itself using its neck frill (see page 35). Make one yourself to see how this special defensive system works.

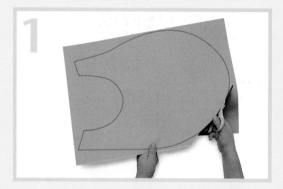

1

Draw one half of the frill shape onto a large sheet of colored cardboard. Use scissors to cut out the shape.

You will need:

- Two large sheets of cardboard
- Pencil
- Scissors
- Tape
- Poster paints
- Paintbrush
- Colored tissue paper
- Glue
- String

2

Make the other half of the frill with another sheet of cardboard. Fold each half like an accordian.

3

Place the two halves together and connect them using tape at one end.

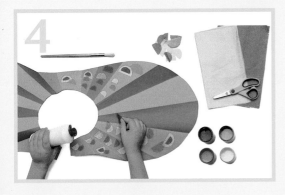

Create a pattern for your cape using paint. Cut out pieces of tissue paper and stick them on using glue to create a scaly texture.

Cut two long pieces of string. Attach them at either end of the cape—to the unpainted side—using tape.

Place the finished cape around your neck and use the string to hold it in position. Give it a tug to raise the frilly cape and scare off your enemies!

Pop-up croc

Create a greeting card

Learn how to cut and fold paper to make your very own pop-up card. Then decorate it for a friend or relative.

You will need:
- Colored cardboard
- Pencil
- Scissors
- Poster paints and paintbrush

Fold the cardboard in half and draw a zigzag line for the croc's teeth. Cut along the line using scissors.

Fold out the teeth shape as shown, so that there is a definite crease. Unfold the cardboard so it lies flat.

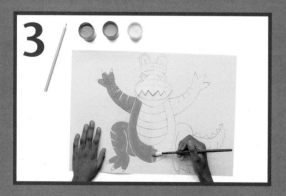

Draw the rest of your croc in pencil and color it with paints. Press out the teeth to make the pop-up work.

Snake stick

Make a slinky snake toy

Snakes have a flexible backbone. Create this model and then use the stick to copy the way a snake coils and slinks over land.

Use a ruler to draw equal strips on the colored cardboard. Use scissors to cut out the strips.

You will need:
- Colored cardboard
- Pencil
- Ruler
- Scissors
- Tape
- Paints
- Paintbrush
- String
- Wooden stick

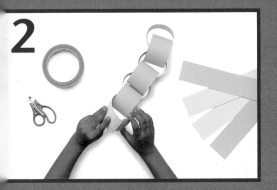

Using tape, make one strip into a loop. Connect other strips on in loops. Add a pointed loop for a tail.

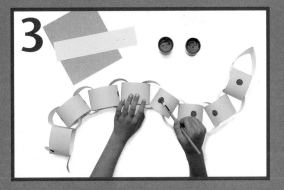

Add eyes and a forked tongue. Paint on markings. Tape one end of string near the head and other end to a stick.

Sticky tongues

Pretend to be a chameleon

Chameleons shoot out their sticky tongues to snatch up juicy insects (see page 26). With this fun game, you can pretend to do the same!

1

Roll up sheets of cardboard to make two tubes—one slightly thinner. Fasten the tubes using tape. Paint the tubes red.

You will need:
- Colored cardboard
- Tape
- Poster paints
- Paintbrush
- Red tissue paper
- Black tissue paper
- White tissue paper
- Double-sided tape
- Scissors

2

Slot the slightly thinner tube inside the larger one. Use tape to hold the two tubes together.

3

Scrunch up lots of red tissue paper into a ball. Add strips of double-sided tape to make it sticky.

4 Push the ball of tissue into the end of the long tube. The double-sided tape should hold it in. This forms the tip of your sticky tongue.

5 Make the flies by scrunching up smaller pieces of black tissue paper. Cut out wing shapes using white paper or tissue paper. Stick them on using tape.

Make two of these sticky tongues. Then put all your flies into a bowl, or on a paper plate, and you are ready to play . . . The person who collects the most flies in one minute is the winning chameleon!

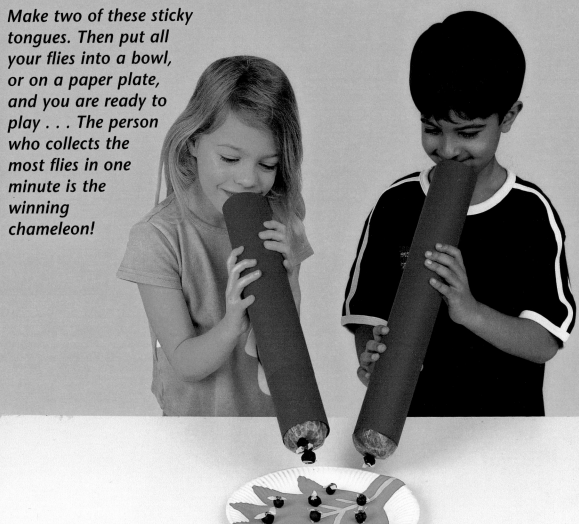

Glossary

ancestor—an animal from which later animals have developed

bask—to sit still in a warm area

breed—to produce young

burrow—to dig a hole to live in

carnivore—meat-eating animal

carrion—the dead bodies of animals

coil—to wind around and around in loops

developing—growing and changing

dew—small drops of water that form during the night on grass and other plants

digest—to break down food so that the body can use it

eardrum—a part of the ear that sends sound vibrations to the inner ear

evolved—changed over time

extinct—when all animals of a certain type have died and none are left

flexible—bendable, stretchy

flipper—limb that is suited for swimming

glide—to float gently through the air

habitat—the area where a plant o animal lives

hatch—to break out of an egg

keratin—a tough, horny substance found in hair, claws, fingernails, and reptiles' skin

mammal—a warm-blooded animal that feeds its young on milk

miniature—tiny

mottled—patterned with different colored patches

nervous system—the network of nerves throughout an animal's body

organ—a part of the body with a special job to do

pierce—to prick and break into or out of

predator—an animal that hunts other animals

prey—an animal hunted by another animal

radio transmitter—a device that sends out signals that can be tracked

ridge—a narrow, raised area on a flat surface

saliva—clear liquid produced in the mouth

skeleton—a framework of bones inside an animal's body

species—a set of animals or plants with the same features

startled—surprised

venomous—full of venom, or poison

wallowing—lying still while floating in water

webbed—webbed feet have toes that are connected by a flap of skin

The content of this book will be useful to help teach and reinforce various elements of the science, language arts, and math curricula in the elementary grades. It also provides opportunities for crosscurricular lessons in social studies, geography, and art.

Extension activities

Writing
What if you could move each of your eyes on its own, like the chameleon on p. 15? How would this ability change your life? Write a short story about how being able to see behind you could help you get out of a difficult situation.

Literature/writing
Read a legend or folk tale about a reptile. Some examples are the legend of Saint George and the Dragon, the Chinese legend of the Great White Snake, and the Australian Aboriginal legend about how the Tortoise lost its tail and teeth. Draw two columns. In one, list ways that the reptile character is like a real animal. In the other, list ways that it is not. (Note: this information could also be displayed on a Venn diagram.)

Math/measurement
Snakes range in length from the thread snake (4 inches, or 10 centimeters) to anacondas and pythons (28 feet, or 8.5 meters, or more). Measure and chalk these lengths on the sidewalk. Research the lengths of several other snakes. Measure, mark, and compare.

Science
The topic of reptiles relates to the scientific themes of diversity, adaptation, structure and function, and behavior. Some specific links to science curriculum content include animal senses (pp. 14–15); classification (pp. 8–9); defense (pp. 12, 20, 24, 34–39); food chains and webs (p. 22, 26–27); growth and development (pp. 13, 30–33); human impact (pp. 40–41), predator/prey relationships (pp. 12, 18–20, 24, 26–27, 34–39); regulation (pp. 10–11); and reproduction (pp. 30–31).

Crosscurricular links

1) Geography/science: Many reptiles are particularly well adapted for desert survival. Use a map to locate deserts in several countries. Research to discover reptiles that live there.

2) Writing, oral language, and art: Choose a reptile you find especially interesting. Use reference materials to write a report. Illustrate it with a large, colorful drawing and give a brief oral report to your classmates.

3) Science/social studies/current events: The Florida Everglades has a serious problem. Some people turned loose their pet pythons when the huge snakes got to be too much to take care of. The snakes multiplied and are changing the whole Everglades ecosystem. They are dangerous to both park animals and visitors. Find out about this situation. Share your information with your classmates or family and discuss what might be done about it.

Using the projects

Children can do these projects at home. Here are some ideas for extending them. Parental supervision is recommended whenever a child is using the Internet.

Page 42: See a live frilled lizard in action! *http://animal.discovery.com/videos/wild-recon-frilled-lizard-on-the-attack.html*

Page 44: pp. 8–9 shows the four different groups of reptiles. Make more greeting cards by drawing an animal from each group on the front and gluing materials such as pieces of torn paper, sandpaper, or sequins to show its skin type.

Page 46: Watch a close-up video of a real chameleon's sticky tongue in action! *http://www.arkive.org/parsons-chameleon/calumma-parsonii/video-08b.html*

Did you know?

- There are more than 8,000 species of reptiles in the world, and they inhabit every continent except Antarctica.

- The king cobra can inject enough poison to kill an elephant.

- Komodo dragons can run at speeds of up to 12 miles (20 kilometers) per hour.

- A snake at a zoo in London, England, was once fitted with a glass eye!

- Marine iguanas sneeze regularly to remove salt in glands near their nose. This salt often lands on their heads, giving them their distinctive white cap.

- Most of the world's snakes (almost two-thirds) are nonvenomous. Only 500 snake species are venomous.

- Geckos are born without eyelids. To stop their eyes from drying out, they lick their eyeballs with their long tongues.

- The shell of a turtle is made up of 60 different bones all connected together.

- Spitting cobras can expel their venom up to 10 feet (3 meters).

- Most snakes can dislocate their jaws to make it easier for them to swallow large prey.

- Reptiles have been around for almost 200 million years.

- You can tell the age of a rattlesnake by counting the rattles on its tail.

- The oldest tortoise ever to have lived was named Tu'i Malila. Born in 1777, it died in 1965, aged 188 years!

- Veiled chameleons have a tongue that is 1.5 times the length of their body.

- The leatherback turtle is the largest turtle species. Adults can grow to an average length of 6.5 feet (2 meters) and weigh up to 1,540 pounds (700 kilograms).

- Crocodiles swallow stones to help grind up food in their stomachs.

Reptiles quiz

The answers to these questions can all be found by looking back through the book. See how many you get right. You can check your answers on page 56.

1) How many species of snakes and lizards are there?
A—100
B—3,000
C—10,000

2) Which is the largest lizard in the world?
A—the marine iguana
B—the anole lizard
C—the Komodo dragon

3) Why do giant tortoises have big feet?
A—to stop them from sinking in sandy ground
B—to help them move faster
C—to help them climb trees

4) What does an armadillo lizard do when it is threatened?
A—it runs away
B—it curls up into a ball
C—it hides its head in the sand

5) How long can a marine iguana stay underwater?
A—30 seconds
B—5 minutes
C—20 minutes

6) What would scientists use to track loggerhead turtles?
A—a cell phone
B—a radio transmitter
C—an undercover detective

7) How many species of venomous lizards are there?
A—10
B—200
C—2

8) What is special about the basilisk lizard?
A—it can run on water
B—it can breathe fire
C—it can fly

9) How do young snakes break out of their eggs?
A—they use their claws
B—they have an "egg tooth" on their upper jaw
C—they wait for the egg to crack

10) What do rattlesnakes do when it gets too cold in the winter?
A—migrate
B—grow thicker skin
C—hibernate

11) What is the most poisonous snake?
A—the sea snake
B—the king cobra
C—the rattlesnake

12) What does the Solomon Island skink eat?
A—insects
B—birds
C—leaves

Books to read

Everything You Need to Know about Frogs and Other Slippery Creatures, DK Children, 2011

Explorers: Reptiles by Claire Llewellyn, Kingfisher, 2011

I Wonder Why Snakes Shed Their Skin by Amanda O'Neill, Kingfisher, 2011

Sea Turtles' Race to the Sea (Fact Finders) by Jennifer Allen Krueger, Capstone Press, 2011

Snakes: Biggest! Littlest! by Sandra Markle, Boyds Mills Press, 2011

The Frog Scientist (Scientists in the Field) by Pamela S. Turner, Sandpiper, 2011

Places to visit

Reptilia Zoo, Ontario, Canada
www.reptilia.org/Zoo.aspx
Reptilia Zoo has many star attractions, including a pair of 23-foot (7-meter)-long pythons. The zoo runs a Junior Keeper program, where children aged 7–13 are given the chance to train as junior reptile zookeepers.

Dinosaur World, Florida
www.dinosaurworld.com/
Visit Dinosaur World and see more than 150 life-size dinosaurs, including brachiosaurus, triceratops, and dilophosaurus.

Cape Fear Serpentarium, Wilmington, North Carolina
www.capefearserpentarium.com
The Cape Fear Serpentarium houses some of the most rare and dangerous reptile species in the world. Watch crocodiles being fed and venomous snakes being handled, and view animals that can be seen nowhere else in captivity.

Websites

What Is a Reptile?
http://kids.yahoo.com/animals/reptiles
This site features a comprehensive description of many reptiles, from long-nosed lizards to mud turtles. It also has information on reptile anatomy, diet, and defense behavior.

Facts about Reptiles
www.buzzle.com/articles/facts-about-reptiles.html
Did you know that some reptiles can run on water? Or that some tortoises live to be more than 120 years old? Learn many more fascinating reptile facts from this website.

National Geographic
http://animals.nationalgeographic.com/animals/reptiles/
This site has many excellent photographs of reptiles, from crocodiles to king cobras. It also has information on the threats posed to endangered reptiles.

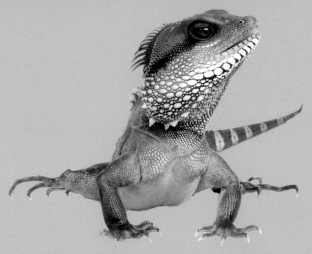

Reptiles quiz answers

1) B	7) C
2) C	8) A
3) A	9) B
4) B	10) C
5) C	11) A
6) B	12) C